The Global Economy and the Environment

The Global Economy and the Environment

David Petechuk

MASON CREST
PHILADELPHIA

Mason Crest
450 Parkway Drive, Suite D
Broomall, PA 19008
www.masoncrest.com

Printed and bound in the United States of America.

CPSIA Compliance Information: Batch #CWI2016.
For further information, contact Mason Crest at 1-866-MCP-Book.

First printing
1 3 5 7 9 8 6 4 2

Library of Congress Cataloging-in-Publication Data

on file at the Library of Congress
ISBN: 978-1-4222-3669-7 (hc)
ISBN: 978-1-4222-8124-6 (ebook)

Understanding Global Trade and Commerce series ISBN: 978-1-4222-3662-8

Table of Contents

KEY ICONS TO LOOK FOR:

Words to Understand: These words with their easy-to-understand definitions will increase the reader's understanding of the text, while building vocabulary skills.

Sidebars: This boxed material within the main text allows readers to build knowledge, gain insights, explore possibilities, and broaden their perspectives by weaving together additional information to provide realistic and holistic perspectives.

Research Projects: Readers are pointed toward areas of further inquiry connected to each chapter. Suggestions are provided for projects that encourage deeper research and analysis.

Text-Dependent Questions: These questions send the reader back to the text for more careful attention to the evidence presented there.

Series Glossary of Key Terms: This back-of-the book glossary contains terminology used throughout this series. Words found here increase the reader's ability to read and comprehend higher-level books and articles in this field.

The north gate of Beijing's Forbidden City is shrouded in smog. Air and water pollution, caused by the country's industrial modernization over the past seventy years, is becoming a major problem for China.

Global Trade and the Environment

I n affluent districts in the city of Beijing, the capital of China, some families are sitting in their homes breathing in fresh Canadian air bottled from Alberta's Banff National Park. The Canadian company that sells the bottled air saw its first shipment of five hundred aluminum bottles of compressed air sell out in four days. The next shipment to China of four thousand bottles sold rapidly as well.

Who are these people in China buying fresh Canadian air? They have come to be referred to as "bubble families," people trying to protect themselves from China's increasingly hazardous air pollution brought on by the country's rapid industrialization in a global economy that has seen international trade and commerce grow to levels never before seen in history. They gained the designation of "bubble families" because they essentially confine themselves to their own homes as much as possible, building "bubbles" of clean air and purified water.

The pollution in some of China's largest industrialized cities, however, has become so bad at times that even being inside is not healthy. In one case, Chinese screenwriter Liu Nanfeng, who is married with a young daughter, had five air purifiers, two air-quality monitors, and a water purification system installed in the family's Beijing apartment. "I feel safe at home, but when we go out to the mall, the indoor and outdoor air are the same," Nanfeng told Alexandra Harney for a Reuters news service article.

 Words to Understand in This Chapter

biodiversity—the variety of life on Earth, including genetic diversity within animal and plant populations, and the variety of habitats in a specific area.

developed country—a country that is industrialized and has a highly diversified economy.

developing country—a country with little industry that is seeking to develop its resources by increased industrialization.

ecosystem—all the living things in a specified area that interact with each other and their nonliving environment, such as the weather, sun, soil, climate, and atmosphere.

greenhouse gases—gases in the atmosphere that absorb infrared radiation from the sun, trap heat in the atmosphere, and increase atmospheric temperatures.

Industrial Revolution—a period in the late-eighteenth century through the nineteenth century in which the predominantly rural, farming societies in Europe and America became industrial and urban.

standard of living—a term that refers to the levels of wealth, comfort, material goods and necessities available to certain segments of society within a particular geographic area.

The pollution in China's cities is so toxic that many people wear masks when outside to protect themselves from particles in the air. Families purchase expensive air purification systems for their homes and stay inside as much as possible.

How Bad Is It?

On Christmas Day 2015, people living in China's largest cities woke up to atmosphere so filled with smog that when they went outside people standing within ten yards (9 m) of them were ghostlike figures, shrouded in haze. Traffic lights and headlights glowed eerily and could barely be seen. Visibility was so poor that the day-after-Christmas flights out of Beijing were canceled. People were warned to stay indoors for health reasons.

Overall, seven of the ten most polluted cities in the world are in China. The country's air pollution problem is thought to be the cause of hundreds of thousands of premature deaths in China each year. China's polluted air, however, does not just affect China. China is the world's largest emitter of *greenhouse gases*, such as carbon dioxide (CO_2), which most climate scientists believe are the driving forces behind global warming.

An Economic Evolution

China is a prime example of how the global economy and international trade and commerce can have both positive and negative effects. For centuries, China was a relatively

 The Population Factor

It took several millennia for the world population to reach 1 billion people. However, over the past two hundred years, the world's population has grown sevenfold, reaching the 7 billion mark in 2011. In 2015, 7.3 billion people occupied the planet. The world population continues to grow at about 80 million people a year. If this growth rate continues, Earth will be home to about 9.2 billion people by 2050.

While it is important to focus on how a global economy affects the environment and the use of the world's natural resources, the growing global population is a critical factor related to environmental issues as well. As the world's population increases and living standards improve, nature is being exploited more and more to meet the needs and wants of this growing population.

In one way, the global economy could help counteract population growth worldwide. Low-income countries have the highest birthrates in the world. As their economies improve, it is expected that population growth rates in these countries will dwindle as families no longer need children to help support families economically. In this sense, a global economy might benefit the environment.

poor country in which the vast majority of people had little opportunity to advance economically. Even as recently as 1978, China's economy was highly regulated and relatively isolated because of bureaucrats in the Chinese Communist Party. As a result, China was still a relatively marginal player in the world trade arena until it began instituting economic reforms in 1979. These reforms ultimately led China to become a member of the World Trade Organization in 2001.

 Did You Know?

Rising air pollution levels in Beijing resulted in a new disease known as "Beijing cough," bouts of sporadic dry coughs or tickles that last from December through April, brought on by the city's severe air pollution. Symptoms typically disappear after people leave the city.

International trade and commerce have grown significantly since the 1970s as part of a growing global economy. Although defined in various ways, a global economy is essentially one characterized by worldwide economic activity among countries around the world. International trade and commerce are fundamental aspects of the global economy and they are also the key factors in the increasing development and prosperity in many parts of the world.

Global economic expansion has conferred many financial benefits on the people of China, primarily in the form of more jobs, higher wages, and a higher *standard of living*. Meanwhile, China has gone through a period of industrialization not seen since the *Industrial Revolution* in the West. China, however, had few environmental regulations, with the ones in place severely outdated. As polluting industries in China grew, and more and more of China's 1.35 billion people could afford cars, China's air pollution became increasingly severe. Finally, in 2014, China announced that it was making the first amendments to its environmental laws in twenty-five years.

It's a Small World After All

In the early 1960s, two staff songwriters for Walt Disney Studios in California, Robert B. Sherman and Richard M. Sherman, wrote a song titled "It's a Small World After All." Although the Sherman brothers were inspired to write a song of peace and brotherhood following the 1962 Cuban Missile Crisis, their song, or at least its title, is more true today than ever before.

Although regional economies are important, the world is operating more and more as a global economy. Throughout much of human history, people have engaged in international trade and commerce. The spice trade among historical civilizations traversed much of the known world at the time. Asia, Northeast Africa, and Europe were all involved in the trade of and for spices such as cinnamon, ginger, pepper, and turmeric. The Great Silk Road was used from around 130 BCE until the Ottoman Empire boycotted trade with the West and closed the various routes in 1453 CE.

However, nearly seven centuries later, advances in high-speed transportation and technologies like the Internet have "shrunk" the world, both in terms of communication

The province of KwaZulu Natal, unique for its rich biodiversity, is one of South Africa's most important farming areas and suppliers of water. But its pristine natural beauty will be threatened if coal mining develops as it has in neighboring Mpumalanga, where the mining industry has had detrimental environmental and social effects, including widespread water pollution.

and international trade. At the same time, countries began to liberalize their economies to take advantage of the growth of international trade and its promising economic benefits. These benefits were wide-ranging, from boosting economies and standards of living to helping create capitalist and democratic political systems in *developing countries*.

Downsides of Globalization

Despite the benefits of a global economy, such an economy has its downsides. Among them is the loss of nonskilled jobs in *developed countries,* such as the United States and Canada, as corporations seek cheap labor in developing nations. A global economy also increases the likelihood that when a single nation experiences economic difficulties economies around the world suffer.

Globalization can have a major impact on the environment as well. As polluting industries grow, the demand for natural resources increases. Large corporations often take advantage of weak environmental regulations in developing nations that have abundant and much-needed natural resources. So the worldwide demand for natural resources is growing at an unprecedented rate, prompting concerns about depletion of these resources.

In addition to worsening air pollution, as seen in China and elsewhere, another environmental issue is the global economy's potential impact on sensitive *ecosystems* and *biodiversity,* that is, the variety of life on the planet. Biodiversity is fundamental to human life. As an example, in 2006 beekeepers and scientists began to notice that the bee population was dying off at an alarming rate, which proved to be a long-term situation. In the United States, 30 percent of the overall bee population has disappeared and almost a third of all bee colonies have perished. In 2014, it was reported that 58 percent of the bee colonies in the province of Ontario, Canada did not survive the winter. Although extremely cold weather was one factor cited in the bees' die-off, poisoning from pesticides was also named as a likely culprit.

Beyond the production of honey, a favorite of humans

Dead bees covered with dust and mites on an empty honeycomb from a hive in decline. Colony collapse disorder (CCD) occurs when most worker bees in a colony die, leaving only the queen and a few nurse bees to care for the queen and her remaining young offspring. No definitive cause has been identified for the dramatic increase in CCD, but a new family of pesticides is one suspect.

and bears, bees figure prominently in the Earth's ecosystems. Our modern diet also relies heavily on the activity of bees, which pollinate about one-sixth of the flowering plant species worldwide and approximately four hundred varieties of agricultural plants. Furthermore, they contribute to the economy, helping to produce agricultural crops worth billions of dollars.

Historically, the decline in biodiversity was largely connected to regional demands for fuel, food, and living space.

Such demands have increased significantly. One reason is the enormous growth in the human population. The other is tied to a globalized economy of international trade. Such trade threatens natural resources as industries develop and the demand for natural resources supporting these industries intensifies.

Industries connected to biodiversity loss include coffee plantations in Mexico, Malaysian palm oil plantations, and Brazilian beef farms. In each of these cases, the industries have grown significantly and cleared more land to meet global demand for their products. The growing Brazilian beef industry, for instance, needed more grazing land for cattle, so ranchers accelerated the deforestation of the Amazon.

Responses to Environmental Concerns

Economic growth in developing countries can lead to stronger environmental regulations, however. Experience has shown that as countries and their populations become wealthier, they both want and can afford to clean up their environment. Economic growth can help countries, such as China, switch to solar and wind power, as well as other renewable energy sources.

As reported in the *Washington Post*, the International Energy Agency announced in March 2015 that, although the world economy grew, greenhouse gas emissions did not increase in 2014. And for the first time in four decades, a halt or reduction in the emission of CO_2 was not associated with an economic downturn, like the one in 2008. Two of the primary reasons, according to the agency, were greater use of renewable energy and increased energy efficiency, with cars becoming more fuel-efficient, for example.

In recent years, the relationship between the environment and global trade has become one of the most complex and contentious issues in world trade policy. Although the emergence of the global economy initially prompted serious environmental concerns, many argue that, over the long term, globalization may actually be good for the environment. That is, if industry is properly regulated and standards of living continue to increase, more and more people may focus less on economic issues and more on environmental issues.

 ## Text-Dependent Questions

1. What was the impact of the Industrial Revolution on the global environment?
2. How do renewable energy and increased energy efficiency help the environment?

 ## Research Project

Choose an endangered habitat and/or animal species and describe the environmental threats to it as well as efforts being made to address the problem or problems. As one example, consider melting ice in Arctic regions that is threatening the polar bear population. Also think about plastic pollution that affects various land- and water-based ecosystems, including the organisms that live in these habitats. Write a two-page report about your chosen topic.

Although petroleum products such as oil and natural gas make life easier, finding, producing, and moving crude oil may have negative effects on the environment, including disruption of both land and marine habitats.

2

The Changing World Economic System

While the rise of the global economy began in earnest during the latter half of the twentieth century, the twenty-first-century global economy is unique in human history. Never before has the world seen economic growth occurring in so many countries around the world. Because the global economy is still in its infancy, its long-term impact on economies, standards of living, and the environment remains uncertain.

International trade has increased to meet the growing consumer demands associated with the economic activity of developing countries. The resulting increase in manufacturing and industries may negatively impact the environment, especially if industries face few environmental regulations. Questions remain, however, about whether or not these effects will increase or decrease over the years with expanded trade.

Will worldwide consumption become so great that polluting industries will permanently damage the environment on both a local and a global scale? Will the global economy lead to a depletion of natural resources? Will multinational corporations and governments take the necessary steps needed to protect the environment? Will the global economy usher in a new era of wealth, part of which will be devoted to environmental protection and the development of environmentally friendly technologies? No one knows.

A Brief History

Trade among countries is not new. International trade dates back to at least the fourth millennium BCE. Scholars believe that civilizations in ancient Mesopotamia and Egypt traded with other communities in Africa and Asia. They exchanged excess food and agricultural products such as wool and textiles for timber, quarried stone, and metal, which Mesopotamia and Egypt lacked.

Throughout most of human history, however, trade among nations has been conducted on a much smaller scale than it is today. During the sixteenth century CE, however, colonization increased dramatically as the nations of

 Words to Understand in This Chapter

imperialist—referring to one government exerting economic power over other governments or territories, often by means of force.

sustainability—the capacity for biological systems to endure, maintaining a diverse environment that remains productive.

A line of monster dump trucks carry 250-ton loads of ore out of an open pit mine. The world's demand for raw materials from natural resources has grown so fast that humankind has consumed more of these resources—from aluminum, copper, and diamonds to sulfur, coal, oil, and natural gas—over the past century than over all the preceding centuries of human existence.

Western Europe, such as Spain, Portugal, England, France, and the Netherlands began exploring and claiming lands in the Americas, Asia, Africa, and the Pacific Ocean. At the same time, *imperialist* business ventures across national borders contributed substantially to these countries' economies.

For example, the British East India Company was founded in Great Britain in 1600 to take advantage of trade in a part of Asia known as the East Indies and eventually

Today, multinational corporations operate manufacturing facilities and sell their products all over the world.

in British colonies in Africa and the Americas as well. The company oversaw the start of the British Empire in India. At one point in its history, the company conducted about half of all world trade in various commodities, from cotton, silk, and indigo dyes to salt, tea, and opium.

The proliferation of corporations doing business on an international scale began in the nineteenth century, prompted by the Industrial Revolution. Companies sought to meet the growing demand for natural resources as manufacturing in the West increased dramatically. These companies were also formed to sell the ever-growing number of products created by various industries.

Following World War II (1939–1945), numerous technological advances accelerated the growth of international investment and trade, especially in Western nations. New advertising outlets, such as television, helped to expand markets around the world. By the 1970s, global commerce related to multinational corporations had reached an unprecedented scale. These multinational corporations sell their products on a global basis and may have their head-

 ## International Trade Organizations

Following World War I (1914–1918), the Great Depression (1929–1939), and World War II (1939–1945), numerous countries began to work together to foster international trade. Organizations were formed to settle disputes and to balance the global marketplace. Examples include the United Nations, the World Bank, and the World Trade Organization (WTO).

The WTO was created in 1947 to both oversee and foster world trade. It establishes and enforces rules for international trade, resolves trade disputes, cooperates with other international economic institutions involved in global economic management, and helps developing countries realize the benefits of the global trading system. For example, the WTO works to help protect the interests of smaller and weaker countries against discriminatory trade practices by larger and more powerful countries.

Encouraging sustainable development and environmental protection are also fundamental goals of the WTO. Although no binding agreements exist for dealing with the environment, WTO has rules that member nations engaged in international trade can adopt to protect the environment. As an example, the WTO Dispute Settlement Body has dealt with disputes concerning turtles that are accidentally captured in the course of commercial fishing in international waters and issues related to air pollution and human health.

quarters in one country and their manufacturing facilities in others.

In 1906, only a handful of multinational corporations had assets of $500 million or more. By 1971, 333 corporations had assets of $1 billion or more. These companies controlled 70–80 percent of world trade outside of state or government planned economies. Today, more than 80,000 multinational companies conduct trade around the world.

Since the mid-1980s, international companies have increasingly invested in less-industrialized nations. They establish factories and businesses in these countries for a number of reasons, from the need for valuable natural resources to the economic benefits of paying lower wages. In addition, many of these countries typically have fewer environmental regulations, meaning that companies could operate with minimal oversight when it came to efforts to protect the environment.

Information Technology and the Global Economy

The rapid rise of information and communications technologies in the twenty-first century has fostered the modern global economy. These technologies include personal computers and software, the Internet, and broadband and wireless communications. Technology has integrated international commerce and changed the internal practices of businesses.

In the first decade of the twenty-first century, business embraced e-commerce, the buying and selling of goods and

Multinational corporations advertise their products at this busy Tokyo intersection.

services or the transmitting of funds and data over an electronic network. According to the Pew Internet & American Life Project, 66 percent of adults around the world have purchased goods online, from books and shoes to airline tickets and Caribbean cruises.

E-commerce has played a major role in helping countries formerly left out of the globally based economy become active participants in international trade and commerce. Conducting business electronically reduces costs, increases efficiency, and removes barriers of time and distance for trade, even for smaller companies. According to a 2013 report by the United Nations Conference on Trade and Development, approximately 1 billion consumers shopped online in 2013. This number is expected to increase significantly going forward. The bottom line is that local economies and the global economy have become increasingly interdependent through the trade of goods and services, as well as the movement of money for investment, trade, or business production purposes.

The new global economy, the increase in the world's population, and higher standards of living for many have combined to create growing worldwide demand for more energy, industries, and goods. Still, the relationship between economic growth and environmental degradation remains controversial. On one side is the belief that the global economy is causing too much harm to the environment. On the other side is the contention that, in the long run, a global economy will benefit the environment as countries and their citizens grow more financially stable.

How Globalization Harms the Environment

The global economy's negative impact on the environment can be traced to numerous sources. These include increased international transport, agriculture and environmentally detrimental land-use practices, industrial processes, waste disposal, and energy production and consumption, such as the burning of fossil fuels such as coal, oil, and natural gas for electricity, heat, and transportation.

Furthermore, more natural resources are required to support the global economy. To obtain these resources, vital ecosystems that support all life on Earth are being damaged. For example, the loss of open land due to industrial and agricultural development is destroying natural habitats crucial to the survival of a wide variety of plant and animal species. Factors involved in this loss of habitat include poisonous toxins introduced into ecosystems and greenhouse gas emissions released into the atmosphere, which contributes to climate change.

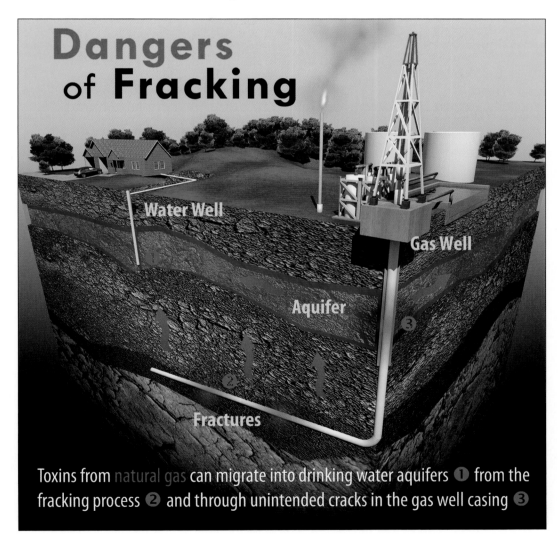

Dangers of Fracking

Water Well

Gas Well

Aquifer

Fractures

Toxins from natural gas can migrate into drinking water aquifers ❶ from the fracking process ❷ and through unintended cracks in the gas well casing ❸

According to a 2016 report by the International Union for Conservation of Nature, nearly 41 percent of all amphibian species and 26 percent of all mammalian species are threatened with extinction. Damage to or the loss of these threatened species also poses a serious threat to human life because wetland ecosystems are nature's way of purifying water. Rain forests are also complex ecosystems that help renew the Earth's air supply by absorbing the greenhouse gas carbon dioxide and producing oxygen in the atmosphere.

In 2015, scientists from Stanford University have found an alarming increase in the rate of extinctions. They discovered that an increase in earthquakes in Oklahoma is likely related to drilling for gas and oil through a process known as "hydraulic fracturing," or fracking. "We are sawing off the limb that we are sitting on," noted Paul Ehrlich, a senior fellow at the Stanford Woods Institute for the Environment in an article for the Stanford News website.

Finally, the goal of a global economy, and capitalism in general, is continued growth, much of which is related to international trade and increased consumption of goods. As more and more people can afford to consume more products, the demand for natural resources and the impact on the environment also increase. And although the world population doubled between 1950 and 2004, the use of wood around the world has more than doubled and the use of coal, oil, and natural gas has increased almost fivefold, according to a 2006 report issued by State of the World.

Yet even those who see the global economy as harmful

to the environment recognize its potential economic bene-fits, especially for developing countries. Nevertheless, many environmentalists argue that new policies to protect the environment have not kept pace with economic growth.

How Globalization Could Help the Environment

Some argue that a better economy will ultimately lead to a better environment. That is, demands for environmental action over the long haul will become stronger as people's standard of living rises and they become more concerned with protecting the environment.

Supporters of globalization contend that, in the long run, both local economies and the global economy depend on a healthy environment and natural resources. As long ago as the nineteenth century, concerns were raised about natural resource scarcity and the potential effects on economies and societies. With advances in science and technology, these effects are better understood today. In response, industry and business are becoming more moti-vated to help preserve the environment and sustain natural resources to keep business thriving.

Those in favor of continued global economic growth also point out that citizens of countries around the world become better informed about environmental issues as their economies become stable and their citizens become wealthier. The environment also benefits from the scientif-ic and technological progress that accompanies economic growth. This progress includes the development of environ-

Recycling programs benefit the environment by keeping items such as electronics from being buried in landfills, where they can emit toxic chemicals that pollute local ecosystems and water supplies. Reusing materials through recycling also reduces to need to extract new raw materials, such as lumber and minerals. For example, a study by the National Recycling Coalition found that when one ton of steel is recycled, it saves 2,500 pounds of iron ore, 1,400 pounds of coal, and 120 pounds of limestone.

mentally friendly production processes and new ways to ensure the *sustainability* of natural resources, such as methods for recycling materials.

When countries and their citizens grow richer, farmers use new technologies that require less land to produce the same amount of food. Marginal land is left fallow, allowing for a more natural ecosystem. Oftentimes, abandoned farmland is made into recreational resources and turned backed into forests or wilderness.

Another argument in support of the global economy is that the governments of wealthier countries are more effective in overseeing environmental protection and conservation efforts. The World Bank in 2007 reported that over time, economic growth in China has prompted the Chinese government to adopt new antipollution regulations and place more emphasis on the sustainability of natural resources, increased energy efficiency, and cleaner manufacturing technologies.

 ## Text-Dependent Questions

1. How has the global economy hurt the environment?
2. What is the relationship between sustainable development and environmental protection?

 ## Research Project

Visit the Ted Talks website and view the video at http://www.ted.com/talks/tim_jackson_s_economic_reality_check?language=en. In this video, economist Tim Jackson talks about his findings concerning the links between lifestyle, societal values, and the environment as they relate to economic growth. Summarize Jackson's viewpoint concerning the environment and economic growth. Then find some opposing viewpoints. How do they differ from Jackson's view? Write a report on your findings.

Most respectable scientists agree that climate change is the greatest humanitarian crisis of our time. It is responsible for rising seas and punishing floods, powerful storms, searing heat, and severe droughts. If unchecked, climate change will threaten the health, economy, and security of human communities.

3

The Global Economy and Climate Change

In the view of many scientists, one of the most crucial environmental issues of the twenty-first century is climate change, especially global warming. According to climate scientists, 2015 was the hottest year since scientists began keeping climate data in 1880. The previous record was set in 2014. A report by the National Oceanic and Atmospheric Administration's National Centers for Environmental Information noted that the record-breaking year was partly due to the effects of a weather pattern known as El Niño. Nevertheless, the report noted that the primary cause of the record-setting heat and ongoing global warming was the emission of greenhouse gases resulting from human activities.

Climate change leading to global warming has been a hot topic of debate for more than two decades. At the center of the debate is whether or not climate change and global warming are caused or made worse by the activities of people and industries. These include greenhouse gas emissions, such as carbon dioxide, produced by the burning of fossil fuels, such as coal and oil.

Other greenhouse gases include methane (CH_4), nitrous oxide (N_2O) and fluorinated gases (F-gases). Methane is released into the atmosphere by agricultural activities, waste disposal, energy use, and the burning of *biomass*. The primary sources of nitrous oxide are agricultural activities, such as the use of fertilizer and the burning of biomass. The release of F-gases is primarily tied to industrial processes, refrigeration, and the use of certain consumer products, such as refrigerants and solvents.

The Threat from Global Warming

According to the National Aeronautics and Space Administration (NASA), 97 percent or more of climate scientists believe that climate-warming trends over the past century are most likely due to human activities, including those related to the growth of a global economy. This belief

 Words to Understand in This Chapter

affluence—an abundance of money, property, and material goods.

biomass—organic matter that comes from living or recently living organisms.

greenhouse effect—the phenomenon of gases in the Earth's atmosphere trapping radiation emitted by the sun, retaining the heat radiated back from the Earth's surface, and raising the overall planetary temperature; the Earth's primary greenhouse gases are water vapor, carbon dioxide, methane, nitrous oxide, and ozone.

is supported by numerous American scientific organizations, including the American Association for the Advancement of Science, the American Chemical Society, the American Geophysical Union, and the American Meteorological Society.

The *greenhouse effect* has some natural causes, and it is important to life on Earth because it keeps the planet from freezing. But the buildup of greenhouse gases can lead to too much warming and result in dangerous outcomes for people and the environment. These effects range from floods and droughts to rising sea levels that threaten coastal cities and towns.

In addition, global warming may compromise the Earth's biodiversity. As an example, animals such as penguins and polar bears live in an environment that is increasingly endangered by warming temperatures and melting ice caps. Scientists have traced the decline of the Adélie penguins in Antarctica over a thirty-year period (1980 to 2010). During that time, the number of breeding pairs fell from 32,000 to 11,000. Global warming also imperils one in five plant species and can affect agricultural production by causing droughts and other weather-related events.

Coral reefs, too, are in danger from global warming, which is raising ocean temperatures and altering the ocean's chemical balance. These effects are not limited to the coral reefs themselves but also threaten the thousands of marine species whose survival relies on these reefs for both food and shelter. In addition, coral reefs are crucial for the global

A large chunk of Arctic ice breaks away from a glacier and falls into the sea. The amount of ice in the Arctic circle has been declining since the 1970s. Scientists believe the melting is caused by higher global temperatures due to greenhouse gas emissions.

economy. The International Coral Reef Initiative has estimated that coral reefs worldwide contribute billions of dollars and millions of jobs to more than one hundred countries around the world.

Ever since the Industrial Revolution, economic development has gone hand in hand with greater consumption of fossil fuels. This situation has continued as the global population has grown and become more affluent, demanding more energy. Increasing industrialization due to the global economy is also accelerating climate change and global warming as more and more fossil fuels are burned by factories, electric power plants, motor vehicles, and individual households.

An article in the journal *Environmental Science & Policy* reported on a study that highlights the relationship between the world's economy and global warming. Researchers from the University of Michigan and the University of Valladolid in Spain pointed out that the worldwide economic collapse in 2008 led to a decrease in the consumption and production of goods and a downturn in international trade. The scientists noted a reduction in atmospheric levels of the greenhouse gas carbon dioxide in 2009, following that economic slowdown.

Did You Know?

Arctic animals are not the only ones threatened by global warming. According to a recent study, global warming is responsible for sheep getting smaller in Scotland.

Global Emissions By Economic Sector

Scientists generally agree that the Earth is undergoing an accelerated rate of warming. Although human sources of greenhouse emissions account for a smaller percentage of such emissions than natural sources, most scientists believe that the natural balance of greenhouse gases in the atmosphere has been upset by human activities, most of which are related to population growth, industrialization, and the global economy.

According to the Center for Climate and Energy Solutions, the primary sources of global greenhouse gas emissions are electricity and heat production, which account for 28 percent of those emissions. These are followed by agricultural activities (14 percent), transportation (12 percent), forestry (12 percent), and manufacturing (12 percent). Overall, energy production of all types accounts for 65 percent of all global greenhouse gas emissions.

The contribution of these various sectors to greenhouse gas emissions varies by country, depending on a wide vari-

 The Cost of Addressing Climate Change

Industries and businesses are starting to respond to climate change and global warming. They are doing this because taking aggressive action to help prevent or lessen the impact of global warming is believed to be less costly than addressing its effects. A 2015 report from Citibank, titled "Energy Darwinism," noted that investing in energy-producing processes that emit fewer greenhouse gases could save the world $41.8 trillion through 2040, compared to the current business-as-usual scenario. The report also observed that doing nothing could result in additional costs of $44 trillion by 2060, because of climate change's negative effects. Overall, according to the Citibank report, addressing global warming could actually boost the global economy and save industries money.

For example, the use of clean energy resources, such as solar power, to increase energy efficiency will benefit certain segments of the economy, such as the renewable energy sector. The price of solar and wind power has fallen significantly in recent years. In some places, like Latin America, renewable energy is becoming cost-effective, while the cost of extracting "dirty" fuels, like coal, has increased. Some estimates indicate that renewable, non-polluting energy sources could contribute up to half of all new electricity generated by 2030.

ety of factors, including population density, standards of living, and industrialization. For example, in Canada, which has a population of approximately 35.7 million and a large energy industry, emissions by economic sector are associated with several key areas of the country's economy. These include oil and gas (25 percent of total emissions), transportation (23 percent), electricity (12 percent), buildings (12 percent), and various emissions-intensive industries (11 percent).

In the United States, which has a population of more than 320 million people, electricity production is the largest source of greenhouse gas emissions, at 31 percent. Transportation accounts for 27 percent, followed by industry (21 percent), commercial and residential buildings (12 percent), and agricultural activities (9 percent).

Affluence and Global Warming

The rise of the global economy and the resulting *affluence* in many countries around the world has boosted the use of natural resources and the various industrial processes that rely on those resources. For example, the burgeoning worldwide economy has prompted increased extraction and burning of fossil fuels. And the world's rain forests are being logged to provide timber, land for cattle grazing and farming, mining, dam construction, oil exploration, and other uses. These rain forests play a crucial role in absorbing CO_2 from the atmosphere and replacing it with oxygen.

The world's forests, soils, and oceans are natural "sinks" that absorb greenhouse gases, a phenomenon known as "carbon sequestration." A major factor that interferes with nature's ability to sequester carbon is waste disposal and how this disposal is managed. A 2010 study, published in the journal *Ambio*, estimated that by the year 2100 even protected environments will experience a decline of about 40 percent in their ability to sequester carbon dioxide. Furthermore, if increased population and economic pressures continue unabated, about one-third of protected lands will be converted to other uses over this same period. As a result, carbon sequestration in the remaining protected areas will be insignificant.

In the United States, the average citizen requires eighteen tons (16,344 kg) of natural resources per year, making the United States among the top ten emitters of greenhouse gases in the world. Although Canada has per capita emissions below the world average, it remains among the top ten emitters as well, largely because the Canadian economy is heavily based on extraction of natural resources. Many researchers believe that global economic growth might push the rest of the world's population to boost their mass consumption to levels rivaling those of the United States, Canada, and Europe. This would significantly increase the volume of greenhouse gases released into the atmosphere.

Another way human consumption and international trade influence the production of greenhouse gases can be seen by examining one multinational corporation. Walmart, the world's largest retailer, has ten thousand stores in twenty-seven countries. The company's activities are associated with 20 billion metric tons of carbon emissions, as much as

Cows produce more of the greenhouse gas methane than the oil industry. An estimated 20 percent of methane gas emissions in the United States is produced by the burps and farts of farmed cattle!

some countries, such as the Dominican Republic and Yemen. Overall, Walmart is approximately the eightieth-largest emitter of carbon in the world.

Walmart has not ignored this impact and has topped the rankings of US-based companies turning to solar energy. The corporation has announced that its goal is to produce zero waste and eventually power nearly all its operations with 100 percent renewable energy.

Good for the Environment, Good for Business

In many instances, industry and business have been reluctant to institute wide-ranging programs to protect the environment. These measures cost money and reduce profits, especially in the short term. However, as scientific evidence mounts concerning human activity and global warming, both governments and industry are taking notice.

New environmental laws and policies are being put in place. Corporations and industries are also looking to stave off environmental damage brought on by global warming, especially in developed countries in the West. These efforts include reducing greenhouse gas emissions. Why are governments and corporations adopting these policies? Because global warming and other environmental crises—including the increase in storms and other catastrophic weather events associated with global warming—are expensive and can negatively affect business and the global economy.

Global warming is also causing a dangerous rise in sea levels, primarily due to the melting of the polar ice caps. Rising sea levels can lead to a loss of land and structural damage to buildings, especially in coastal towns and cities.

The British government's *Stern Review on the Economics of Climate Change*, published in 2006, points out that global warming can potentially have serious impacts on water resources, food production, health, and the environment. And the cost of dealing with these crises could lower global gross domestic product (GDP) by at least 5 percent each year far into the future.

The GDP represents the size of an economy in terms of the total monetary value of all goods and services produced over a certain period. It is a leading indicator used by economists to determine the size and health of an economy. Although certain segments of the economy may reap profits from dealing with the impacts of global warming, the global economy in general will suffer from its impacts on production and consumption. According to some estimates, the continuing impact of climate change and global warming could reduce global GDP by more than 20 percent by 2100.

Text-Dependent Questions

1. What economic event may have caused a reduction in atmospheric levels of the greenhouse gas carbon dioxide in 2009?
2. What is carbon sequestration?
3. What is the total amount of Walmart's annual carbon emissions?

Research Project

Go to NASA's Global Climate Change app website at http://climate.nasa.gov/earth-apps/. Use the ClimateTime Machine app to research how climate indicators are changing over time in relation to sea ice, sea level, carbon dioxide, and global temperature. Write a report about your findings.

A worker attempts to clean oil from a beach at Koh Samet, Thailand. In 2013, an under-sea crude oil pipeline burst, spilling at least 13,000 gallons (50,000 liters) of oil and possibly as much as 58,800 gallons (200,000 liters) onto nearby beaches and resort areas. Such spills greatly harm populations of local marine life and seabirds.

A Healthier Global Economy

Businesses, politicians, governments, and segments of the general population often view environmental protection policies as harmful to both individual businesses and economic competitiveness as a whole. In the short term, pollution regulations and the costs associated with them may cut down on company profits and the ability to expand trade, both on a local and a global scale. This is especially true during difficult economic times.

Growing environmental awareness, however, dating back to the 1960s, spawned the field of environmental economics. This discipline examines the relationship among long-term economic health, environmental protection, and natural resource sustainability. Some recent environmental economics studies have noted that, over the long term, economies do not suffer as a result of stronger environmental policies and regulations. On the contrary, environmental *stewardship* and natural resource sustainability ultimately may improve economies.

For example, *wetlands* serve as natural levees, protecting and limiting the damage caused by storms, such as hurricanes. A 2008 study, published in *Ambio*, placed the value of the coastal wetlands of the United States at $23.2 billion. It is also estimated that US wetlands are fundamentally important to the health of the country's multibillion-dollar commercial and recreational fishing industries. On a global basis, the total economic value of wetlands around the world has been estimated at $3.4 billion per year. Wetlands in Asia have the highest economic value, at $1.8 billion per year.

In terms of climate change and global warming, the DARA group and the Climate Vulnerable Forum noted in 2012 that climate change was already contributing to nearly 400,000 deaths a year and costing the world economy more than $1.2 trillion annually. They found the impacts are greatest in developing countries. The study was

 Words to Understand in This Chapter

carbon footprint—the amount of greenhouse gases produced to support human activities, typically expressed in equivalent tons of carbon dioxide.

green economy—an economy that strives to reduce threats to the environment and avoids ecological scarcities while fostering sustainable development.

infrastructure—fundamental organizational and physical structures and facilities, such as buildings, roads, and power supplies necessary for the operation of an enterprise or society.

stewardship—an ethic that involves the responsible planning and management of resources.

wetlands—land consisting of marshes or swamps, and wet, spongy soil.

endorsed by more than fifty scientists, economists, and policy experts and commissioned by twenty governments.

Policy Reform

According to a 2010 study, titled "Economics of Ecosystems and Biodiversity," the global economic and financial systems need reform to protect and sustain the environment while helping the global economy to flourish. In the past, environmental protection efforts were largely nation-based. The United States and Canada each had its own environmental protection policies and laws, while places such as China, India, and various developing countries had their own policies, which were typically much weaker than those put in place by Western countries.

 Did You Know?

According to the United Nations, the countries most likely to reach complete economic sustainability in connection with natural resources, production, and consumption are Sweden, Norway, Denmark, Finland, and Switzerland.

Today, environmental issues such as global warming have prompted more efforts at establishing international environmental policies and recommendations. Although it is ultimately up to individual nations to agree to these policies and recommendations, these policies typically involve negotiations on how to protect the environment while not diminishing trade and not hurting national economies.

In general, environmental policies and regulations concerning the global economy and international trade are developed by governments, often working in collaboration with intergovernmental agencies, such as the United Nations. For example, the United Nations and its some of its members developed the Montreal Protocol on Substances Depleting the Ozone Layer. This international treaty set goals to phase out the use of substances responsible for ozone depletion, which can cause human health problems from overexposure to the sun's ultraviolet radiation. As of June 2015, all member countries of the United Nations and the European Union have ratified the original protocol.

The treaty has been amended over the years and applies to all countries that ratified the protocol. These amendments focus on speeding up the phasing out of ozone-depleting substances. Kofi Annan, former secretary general of the United Nations, called the Montreal Protocol "perhaps the single most successful international agreement to date," wrote Elizabeth Kolbert in the *New Yorker*.

Individual government policies can have a global impact as well. For example, Canada is developing environmental policies that target both its own economy and the global economy. Because of its abundance of natural resources, such as oil and forests, Canada is a country ripe to take advantage of the global economy. In addition to efforts to reduce Canada's collective *carbon footprint*, Prime Minister Justin Trudeau pledged in 2015 that Canada would contribute $2.65 billion over five years to help developing countries reduce greenhouse gas emissions and adapt to climate change.

Plastic bottles require oil to produce, and pollute the environment. There is also concern that chemicals from the bottles can leach into groundwater.

Nongovernmental Organizations

In addition to individual governments and intergovernmental organizations, nongovernmental organizations (NGOs) also play a role in developing such policies. This role includes serving as advocates for environmental regulation, helping in the collection and dissemination of information, consulting on policy development, and conducting assessment and monitoring efforts.

NGOs, which include international companies, typically have no official regulatory or formal powers over international decision-making processes. Nevertheless, their

Christina Figueres, executive secretary of the United Nations Framework Convention on Climate Change, speaks at the 2016 Investor Summit on Climate Risk. The event was co-hosted by United Nations Foundation, Ceres and the United Nations Office for Partnerships.

influence may be tremendous. NGOs have successfully promoted new environmental agreements both within nations and internationally.

Historically, NGOs are most effective when they work together in coalitions, pooling their resources, and coordinating their lobbying efforts. For example, the Ceres Coalition is made up of more than 130 institutional and socially responsible investors, environmental and social advocacy groups, and other public interest organizations, as well as Fortune 500 companies. The coalition promotes sustainability in a global economy by influencing companies, policy makers, and other market players to incorporate environmental and social factors into their decision making. It also mobilizes investors and business leaders to build a thriving, sustainable global economy in the process.

Ceres and the United Nations Foundation held the first Investor Summit on Climate Risk in 2003, during which a group of investors launched the Investor Network on Climate Risk. The network helped foster investor interest in climate change and prompted company shareholder resolutions that sought better disclosure from oil, gas, and electric companies concerning their impact on climate risks and their strategies to reduce these risks. In 2014, Ceres launched a corporate call to action on climate change that has prompted more than 750 companies to sign a declaration acknowledging the importance of climate change and the need for a bold response to it. The declaration also noted that reducing the overall carbon footprint of corporations offers enormous economic opportunity.

According to the International Energy Agency, governments globally spend $409 billion subsidizing the fossil fuel industry.

Developing Countries and Past Mistakes

In a global economy, developing countries, with their relatively low incomes, are less likely than more developed nations to address environmental issues and place strong constraints on growth to protect the environment as their economies grow. The World Health Organization estimates that in India outdoor air pollution causes approximately 527,700 deaths a year. In Mexico, economic growth has created a host of environmental issues, including destruction of natural habitats and chemical pollution from factory discharges and waste dumping. Malaysia's developing economy led to deforestation, a growing endangered species list, and unsafe levels of air pollution. Deforestation in Malaysia stems from timber and palm oil plantations, and construction of new roads and housing developments.

Developing countries, however, are starting to address environmental concerns. In 1996 the Mexican government formed the Secretariat of the Environment, Natural Resources, and Fisheries, and staffed the organization with respected environmentalists. In 2013 the government reacted to growing smog and air pollution by announcing that it was going to institute stricter fuel economy standards for its cars, in hopes of reducing the amount of pollution from motor vehicle exhaust.

Other developing countries, in Asia, the Middle East, and Latin America, are also examining ways to update and strengthen their environmental laws. Some of these nations have imposed jail time and fines for pollution incidents. In

Wind farms, such as this one in Spain, provide clean energy at a relatively low cost. According to the US Department of Energy, in 2014, more than $8 billion of private capital was invested in the U.S. economy to build wind-energy projects that and employed more than 73,000 workers.

2011, for example, India drafted two new laws calling for environmental remediation of land used in strip mining.

A Global Green Economy

According to the United Nation's report *World Economic and Social Survey 2013*, sustainable development will require global actions to ensure economic progress while simultaneously strengthening environmental protection.

In Mexico City, the Bus Rapid Transit (BRT) program was developed to reduce heavy congestion on city streets. Over the past few years, these electric-powered buses have reduced commuting times and air pollution while also improving access to public transit for poorer residents. With government assistance, the program is being expanded to other Mexican cities.

These efforts will also have to focus on the needs of developing countries' poorest and most vulnerable populations. To address these issues, consumption and consumption patterns must change and governments must strengthen laws requiring private companies to refrain from causing environmental degradation. One way to do this is to move toward a global *green economy*, one that strives to reduce environmental risks and promote sustainable development without harming the environment. In its 2011 report, titled

Towards a Green Economy: Pathways to Sustainable Development and Poverty Eradication, the United Nations Environment Programme (UNEP) noted that such an economy is "one in which material wealth is not delivered . . . at the expense of growing environmental risks, ecological scarcities and social disparities."

 NAFTA and the Environment

Trade agreements among countries are designed to boost the economies of participating countries, but they do not always achieve that goal or bode well for the environment. For example, the 1994 North American Free Trade Agreement (NAFTA) between Canada, Mexico, and the United States was touted as a win-win situation, both economically and environmentally, for all involved. Neither of these promises panned out as expected, especially in Mexico.

More than 2,700 maquiladoras, or factories with equipment purchased on a duty-free basis, were established in Mexico in the years following the agreement. These factories focus on export-oriented manufacturing and assembly plants. The economic benefits of these operations have primarily gone to investor groups and countries outside of Mexico. In addition, most of the factories were constructed near the environmentally strained and highly populated border between Mexico and the United States. These factories have boosted the population in already overcrowded cities, created sewage and waste disposal problems, and exacerbated air pollution because of increased traffic.

A 2014 report by the Sierra Club estimated that greenhouse gas emissions in the region increased from 7 billion metric tons in 1990 to approximately 8.3 billion tons in 2005. "Government must take a page out of the history books and stop negotiating trade pacts that gut protections for our air, water, land, workers, and communities," Ilana Solomon, director of the Sierra Club's Responsible Trade Program, told Huffington Post website contributor Michael McAuliff.

Environmental concerns and regulations are sparking innovations in clean technologies and prompting industries to focus more on developing nonpolluting technologies and sources of energy, known collectively as "green technologies." One of the main obstacles to "going green" in a global economy is that such policies need to be designed and implemented on a global basis.

At this point, international organizations are developing guidelines to foster a green economy and green growth. In addition to UNEP, these organizations include the World Bank, the Organization for Economic Cooperation and Development, and the Global Green Growth Institute.

In his book *Greening the Global Economy*, Robert Pollin argues that investing in renewable energy and energy efficiency to reverse global warming would be money well spent. According to his calculations, it would cost about $1.5 trillion to adequately address global warming, whereas worldwide spending to counter global warming as of 2015 was only around $450 billion. Pollin admits the $1 trillion in extra costs seems astronomical, but insists that the ultimate result would be phenomenal growth in well-paying, green energy jobs.

Pollin claims that China and India, which have resisted addressing pollution, would experience a net increase in well-paying jobs of 6.4 million and 5.7 million, respectively, by investing in renewable energy resources, such as wind and solar power. In the United States, investing a mere 1.5 percent of the gross domestic product would create 1.5 million clean energy jobs. Overall, according to some estimates, the net increase in jobs would be around 650,000 after taking into account job losses in the fossil fuel industries.

Canada has ranked among the top ten countries in terms of clean tech innovation. Still, finding investors for green companies has been difficult. Some government and energy industry groups, such as the Canadian Association of Petroleum Producers (CAPP), have stated that Canada's oil extraction industry will fuel job growth for many years. Yet CAPP also acknowledges that the oil business will not create as many jobs by 2035 as efforts in other economic sectors, including the green economy sector.

Moving to more green-oriented agricultural methods would also create jobs and reduce pressure on the environment, as well as enhancing food security and improving nutrition and health, especially in developing countries. According to UNEP, green investments in water-dependent ecosystems, water *infrastructure*, and water management will result in more efficient water use and increased agricultural production.

UNEP believes a greening economy is also a win-win situation for the industrial sector as a whole by increasing biofuel and industrial production. Natural resource scarcity is becoming a serious issue for many industries. Reserves of easily recoverable oil are diminishing, and it is becoming more expensive to access these reserves. The amount of high-quality metal ores is also diminishing. Technologies to optimize resource efficiency, improvements in productivity methods, and recycling could all offset the specter of limited natural resources

A booth at the Ecobuild trade show in London. Ecobuild is an annual conference for the construction and energy market that provides information about sustainable design and environment-friendly building practices.

Looking to the Future

In the final analysis, a green economy does not replace efforts at sustainable development in some current industries. However, according to UNEP, it is becoming increasingly clear that achieving sustainability rests on changing economies both locally and globally.

Not everyone, however, comes out a winner in the short term during a transition to a green economy and sustainable development. For example, in the fossil fuel industry, company failings and job losses will affect many workers and their families. Among other challenges are establishing a green infrastructure and transitioning the world's growing industrial base to a green economy.

The relationship between the global economy and the global environment continues to be studied by economists, scientists, and environmentalists. In response, not only will business and industry likely undergo significant changes, but consumers will also play a role in fostering an environmentally friendly global economy through their consuming habits. Governments, nongovernmental organizations, industries, and businesses will have to work together to help smooth the way for a global economy that is good for the environment, good for the global economy, and good for all life on Earth.

 ## Text-Dependent Questions

1. What can be done about globalization's negative impacts?
2. How can nongovernmental organizations, which have no regulatory power, help foster the global economy and environmental protection?

 ## Research Project

The Kyoto Protocol is an international agreement to reduce greenhouse gas emissions associated with global warming, based on the belief that global warming is largely due to human-made emissions. Write a two-page report about the Kyoto Protocol, explaining why the United States never ratified the agreement and/or why Canada withdrew from the protocol in 2012. You might also comment on the difficulties of forging major international agreements.

Organizations to Contact

Canadian Business for Social Responsibility
145 Front Street, E #102
Toronto, Ontario M5A1ES, Canada
Phone: +1 416-703-7435
Fax: +1 426-703-7475
Email: info@cbsr.ca
Website: www.iclei.org

US Chamber of Commerce
1615 H Street, NW
Washington, DC 20062
Phone: (202) 659-6000
Fax: (202) 463-3126
Email: Americas@uschamber.com
Website: www.uschamber.com

US Environmental Protection Agency
1200 Pennsylvania Avenue, NW
Washington, DC 20460
Phone: (202) 272-0167
Website: www3.epa.gov

United Nations Environment Programme
United Nations Avenue, Gigiri
PO Box 30552, 00100
Nairobi, Kenya
Phone: (254-20) 7621234
Email: unepinfo@unep.org
Website: www.unep.org

World Bank
1818 H Street NW
Washington DC 20422
Phone: 202-473-1000
Fax: 202-477-6931
Website: www.worldbank.org

World Trade Organization (WTO)
Centre William Rappard
Rue de Lausanne 154
CH-1211 Geneva 21
Switzerland
Phone: +41 (0)22 739-5111
Fax: +41 (0)22 731-4206
Email: enquiries@wto.org
Website: www.wto.org

Series Glossary

barter—the official department that administers and collects the duties levied by a government on imported goods.

bond—a debt investment used by companies and national, state, or local governments to raise money to finance projects and activities. The corporation or government borrows money for a defined period of time at a variable or fixed interest rate.

credit—the ability of a customer to obtain goods or services before payment, based on the trust that payment will be made in the future.

customs—the official department that administers and collects the duties or tariffs levied by a government on imported goods.

debt—money, or something else, that is owed or due in exchange for goods or services.

demurrage—extra charges paid to a ship or aircraft owner when a specified period for loading or unloading freight has been exceeded.

distributor—a wholesaler or middleman engaged in the distribution of a category of goods, esp to retailers in a specific area.

duty—a tax on imported goods.

export—to send goods or services to another country for sale.

Federal Reserve—the central bank of the United States, which controls the amount of money circulating in the US economy and helps to set interest rates for commercial banks.

import—to bring goods or services into a country from abroad for sale.

interest—a fee that is paid in exchange for the use of money that has been borrowed, or for delaying the repayment of a debt.

stock—an ownership interest in a company. Stocks are sold by companies to raise money for their operations. The price of a successful company's stock will typically rise, which means the person who originally bought the stock can sell it and earn a profit.

tariff—a government-imposed tax that must be paid on certain imported or exported goods.

value added tax (VAT)—a type of consumption tax that is placed on a product whenever value is added at each stage of production and at final sale. VAT is often used in the European Union.

World Bank—an international financial organization, connected to the United Nations. It is the largest source of financial aid to developing countries.

Further Reading

Crayton, Lisa. *Globalization: What It Is and How It Works.* New York: Enslow, 2016.

David, Laurie, and Cambria Gordon. *The Down to Earth Guide to Global Warming.* New York: Orchard Books, 2007.

Larkin, Amy. *Environmental Debt: The Hidden Costs of Changing Global Economy.* New York: St. Martin's Press, 2013.

Pollin, Robert. *Greening the Global Economy.* Cambridge, MA: MIT Press, 2015.

Rivoli, Pietra. *The Travels of a T-Shirt in the Global Economy: An Economist Examines the Markets, Power, and Politics of World Trade.* Hoboken, NJ: John Wiley & Sons, 2015.

United Nations Environment Programme. *Towards a Green Economy: Pathways to Sustainable Development and Poverty Eradication.* Nairobi, Kenya: UNEP, 2011.

Internet Resources

www.globalissues.org
The website of the World Resources Institute includes information on natural resources in relation to economic opportunity and human well-being.

http://www.iss.nl
The Political Economy of Resources, Environment and Population research group provides information on poverty, environmental issues, and resource sustainability in relation to the global economy.

www.trade.gov
The official site of the International Trade Administration includes information on global markets, industries and industry analysis, and data on enforcement of and compliance with trade agreements.

www.washingtonpost.com
The online presence of the Washington Post includes articles about the global economy and the environment.

Publisher's Note: The websites listed on this page were active at the time of publication. The publisher is not responsible for websites that have changed their address or discontinued operation since the date of publication. The publisher reviews and updates the websites each time the book is reprinted.

Index

About the Author

David Petechuk is a freelance writer and former director of publications at a major US medical center.

Other Environmental Impacts

Besides climate change and global warming, brought on by greenhouse gas emissions, other areas of environmental concern are also associated with the global economy and increased international trade. These include various forms of pollution, depletion of natural resources, and species extinction.

While the phenomenal increase in the human population has figured prominently in these issues, the World Economic Forum believes that population growth over the coming decades will have a far less significant impact on the environment than global economic growth and development. For example, it is projected that China, with its burgeoning *middle class*, will be responsible for just 4 percent of the world's estimated population growth over the coming years but will be the source of approximately 40 percent of the demand for more energy.

Air Pollution

The various polluting activities associated with growing industry and international trade affect the air, water, and land. For example, air pollution from power plants, factories, and cars burning fossil fuels can cause "acid rain." Acid rain occurs when gases such as nitrogen oxide and sulfur dioxide react with droplets of water to form nitric and sulfuric acids and then fall back to the Earth in the form of rain or other precipitation. This has detrimental environmental effects on soil, forests, and water.

Environmental regulations, such as the 1990 US Clean Air Act and the Canada-United States Air Quality Agreement of 1991, have reduced acid rain in North America. Many North American lakes and waterways are still trying to recover from acid rain that fell before these measures were put in place, and they're striving to become fully habitable for marine and other species. Acid rain remains a significant problem in other parts of the world as well.

 Words to Understand in This Chapter

middle class—the group in a society that is between the upper and working classes, typified by professional and business workers.

stratosphere—the second layer of the Earth's atmosphere about six miles (9.5 km) above the Earth's surface.

ultraviolet (UV) radiation—invisible rays that are part of the energy that comes from the sun.

Another atmospheric issue is ozone depletion. Ozone is a gas that occurs both at ground level and in the Earth's upper atmosphere, or *stratosphere*. It can be harmful to the health of both humans and animals at ground level. In the stratosphere, however, ozone protects organisms on Earth from the sun's *ultraviolet (UV) radiation*, which, in unusually large amounts, can cause skin cancer and cataracts and impair the human immune system.

Ozone-depleting substances are primarily human-made and include chlorofluorocarbons, hydrochlorofluorocarbons, and halons, substances formerly used and sometimes still used in coolants, fire extinguishers, solvents, pesticides, and as foaming agents and aerosol propellants. These substances can thin out the "good" ozone in the stratosphere, allowing increased amounts of UV radiation to reach the Earth. In addition to serious health effects on humans, ozone depletion can damage sensitive crops, leading to lower crop yields, and damage forests and other plant life by increasing their susceptibility to disease, pests, and environmental stresses, such as harsh weather. If unregulated, increased use of ozone-depleting substances could become increasingly problematic.

Water Pollution

Pollution of the oceans and waterways is the most pressing environmental problem in the world today, according to some studies. Industrial wastes, which accumulate in lakes and rivers, are a main source of water pollution. Many of these wastes are toxic to some marine life and the animals that eat these plants and creatures. In addition, microbial pollutants from sewage can result in infectious diseases in aquatic life and harm animals and humans who drink the water. It also can reduce the amount of potable water that is safe for human consumption.

Emissions into the air from power plants, motor vehicles, and other sources can also contribute to water pollution by accelerating a process known as eutrophication, in which high concentrations of nutrients, such as nitrogen, stimulate blooms of algae in the water. These blooms, if significant, can deplete oxygen from the water and suffocate fish and other aquatic organisms. This condition occurs naturally in some aging bodies of water, but human activities can significantly accelerate the process.

Nonrenewable Resources

A key issue connected with globalization and increasing consumption is the depletion of the Earth's natural resources, especially nonrenewable resources. These are resources that have economic value but cannot be readily replaced by natural means to meet consumption demands because their formation typically requires billions of years.

Nonrenewable resources include gas, oil, and coal, all of which are the primary sources of energy throughout the world. Minerals and metal ores are also nonrenewable resources and are in high demand for a variety of uses, including applications in the nuclear, chemical, metallurgical, construction, rubber, and textile industries, to name just a few. The current supply of most of these resources is

Aerial view of an enormous open-pit copper mine in Chile. Mining processes can leave vast scars on the landscape, and can contaminate the local ecology through the release of toxic chemicals used in the process of extracting precious metals from ore.

relatively abundant. However, increased demands on these resources could mean supplies will run out for future generations. Among the minerals used by industry and consumers, whose supplies are expected to decline in coming years, are gas, zinc, aluminum, coal, and iron.

One study conducted in Australia and published in the journal *Resources Policy* noted that most mineral resources throughout the world will not be in serious decline or exhausted in the near future. However, the study found that the global extraction and processing of these minerals is becoming more complicated. To access these minerals and ores, the mining industry has to dig more deeply, at an increased cost. So these resources will no longer be easy and cheap to gather but will, instead, require more complex and expensive extraction processes. Furthermore, sustainability of these resources far into the future remains unknown.

Another factor to take into account is the effect that securing nonrenewable resources through mining, drilling, and other processes has on the environment. Oil spills during drilling operations have made headlines throughout the world. Mining also has had disastrous environmental impacts. For example, open pit mining (a process in which material is excavated from an open pit) can expose miners to radioactive elements and metallic dust. Pit mines produce tailings—ground rock, and process effluents (liquid or sewage wastes) generated in a mine's processing plant. These tailings include toxic and radioactive elements that can leak into bedrock, rivers, and streams if not properly contained. Underground mining can also release toxic compounds into the air and the groundwater.

Renewable Resources

Forests, plants, and animals are considered renewable natural resources. This means they can be replenished both naturally and through human efforts, such as by planting trees, in a relatively short time. Energy from the sun and wind is also considered a renewable resource. Sun and wind as energy resources differ from other renewable

It is estimated that about one-third of human-related carbon emissions gets absorbed by global forests each year. However, many rain forest areas in the Amazon and the Pacific are being heavily logged, and this deforestation reduces the overall capacity of the remaining forests to trap carbon from human emissions.

resources in that they are in relatively constant supply and, for the most part, not affected by human use.

The overuse of other renewable resources can have serious environmental consequences, however. Not only are trees and forests a source of energy production—think wood-burning stoves and fireplaces—they are also used for building materials and numerous other products. According to the World Wildlife Fund, forests play a major

A Conservation Pioneer

Sustainable use of natural resources is not a new idea. In the United States, one of the first to emphasize this was Gifford Pinchot, an American forester who served as the first chief of the US Forest Service from 1905 to 1910.

Pinchot championed the controlled yet profitable use of forests and other natural resources. He also helped establish the conservation movement, together with President Theodore Roosevelt. In his 1910 book *The Fight for Conservation*, Pinchot asked this question: "Shall we conserve . . . resources, and in our turn transmit them, still unexhausted, to our descendants?"

Pinchot went on to write: "When the natural resources of any nation become exhausted, disaster and decay in every department of national life follow as a matter of course. Therefore the conservation of natural resources is the basis, and the only permanent basis, of national success." Although Pinchot was addressing the situation in the United States, his warning applies more than ever before to the global economy and society.

role in the growing global economy. The forest industry is responsible for more than $186 billion in global trade, primarily based on wood products used by industries and middle-class consumers around the world.

Forests are an integral part of the world's environment. Forests, especially rain forests in tropical climates, act as a stabilizing force by reducing the amount of carbon dioxide in the atmosphere. It is estimated that deforestation, especially the cutting down of tropical rain forests, accounts for a 12–17 percent increase in greenhouse gas emissions.

The global demand for tropical hardwoods has become

an $8-billion-a-year industry. In 2013, the Amazon Conservation Association learned of rain forests being cut down deep in the jungle. When association members began to investigate this deforestation, they thought the destruction of forests was minimal. However, by 2015, the destruction had grown from just a few acres to nearly 5,000 acres (2,000 ha). According to the association, the loss was related to one specific company that was looking to become the largest producer of inexpensive cocoa.

According to a 2008 article in *New Scientist*, one study of the Brazilian Atlantic rain forest found that certain aspects of the forest can recover their vitality within sixty-five years. Still, it might take up to four thousand years for the rain forest to regain its full biodiversity. Almost all types of forests do not regenerate well when large areas are logged, and the soil is damaged or removed and erosion occurs. Rain forests are especially vulnerable to logging damage because their ecosystem is so complex.

Logging is not restricted to tropical rain forests alone. Globally, the world has been losing forests at the rate of forty-eight football fields per minute. Deforestation is the greatest in some of the world's most biologically diverse areas, from the Amazon and Sumatra to Borneo and eastern Russia. Overall, nearly 50 percent of the world's original forests have been lost. If the current rate of tropical forest loss continues, it is estimated that tropical forests will no longer exist by 2100.

Not all the news is bad, however. In 2015 the United Nations Food and Agriculture Organization found that the rate of deforestation had recently slowed, especially compared to the 1990s. Yet some critics have observed that the data supporting this slowdown has been supplied by local governments with varying abilities to determine net forest loss. Another study, published in *Geophysical Resource Letters*, found that forest loss in the tropics accelerated overall by 62 percent from 1990 to 2010.

Economic Growth and Sustainability

By 2050, humans could consume an estimated 140 billion tons (64 billion kg) of minerals, ores, fossil fuels, and biomass, a threefold increase over current demands. The United Nations Environment Programme noted that, given the finite nature of these resources, the concern is that these resources will be unsustainable over the long run.

As an example, consider the demand for valuable natural resources in the Arctic. Densely populated countries and parts of the world, such as Japan, Korea, and the European Union, have minimal local access to many of the resources that are readily found in the Arctic.

The northern regions of the Earth are prime resources for some fishing industries. The Bering Sea is one of the richest fisheries on Earth, but overfishing ended up putting an end to pollock fishing in the area in 1992. In addition, overfishing by international fishing fleets can have a negative impact on a marine ecosystem. However, there have been conflicting reports as to whether or not commercial fishing and overfishing irreparably deplete stocks enough to profoundly compromise the marine ecosystem.

By 2030 the world's population and the global economy are expected to require 50 percent more food, 45 percent more energy, and 30 percent more freshwater. Meanwhile, it is becoming increasingly clear that a healthy environment is a prerequisite for a healthy global economy, which needs the natural resources the Earth provides. So most agree that policies to conserve natural resources and protect the environment must be put in place.

 ## Text-Dependent Questions

1. What are the differences between renewable and nonrenewable natural resources?
2. What dangers do tropical rain forests currently face?

 ## Research Project

Compare indoor air and pollution with outdoor air and pollution in your area. Take two white index cards and write "INDOOR AIR" on one and "OUTDOOR AIR" on the other. Smear petroleum jelly on the middle of each card. Put the "INSIDE" card on a flat surface inside your home in an open room. Put the "OUTSIDE" card on a flat surface outside, such as on a table, and secure it by placing a heavy object on the edge of the card. (Put it in a place sheltered from rain or snow.) Examine the sticky area on the cards after about a week. You will see many fine particles on each one. Explain where they come from on the inside as opposed to the outside.

Increased use of renewable energy, such as wind and solar power, can reduce harmful carbon emissions.